Empathy

Julie Murray

Abdo Kids Junior
is an Imprint of Abdo Kids
abdobooks.com

Abdo
CHARACTER EDUCATION
Kids

abdobooks.com

Published by Abdo Kids, a division of ABDO, P.O. Box 398166, Minneapolis, Minnesota 55439.

Abdo Kids Junior™ is a trademark and logo of Abdo Kids.

Printed in the United States of America, North Mankato, Minnesota.

102019

012020

Photo Credits: iStock, Shutterstock

Production Contributors: Teddy Borth, Jennie Forsberg, Grace Hansen

Design Contributors: Christina Doffing, Candice Keimig, Dorothy Toth

Library of Congress Control Number: 2019941190

Publisher's Cataloging-in-Publication Data

Names: Murray, Julie, author.

Title: Empathy / by Julie Murray

Description: Minneapolis, Minnesota : Abdo Kids, 2020 | Series: Character education | Includes online resources and index.

Identifiers: ISBN 9781532188664 (lib. bdg.) | ISBN 9781644942741 (pbk.) | ISBN 9781532189159 (ebook) | ISBN 9781098200138 (Read-to-Me ebook)

Subjects: LCSH: Empathy--Juvenile literature. | Compassion--Juvenile literature. | Emotions--Social aspects--Juvenile literature. | Moral ideas--Juvenile literature.

Classification: DDC 152.41--dc23

Table of Contents

Empathy

Empathy is **understanding** the feelings of another.

It is showing that you care.

Nora is sad. Her mom hugs her.

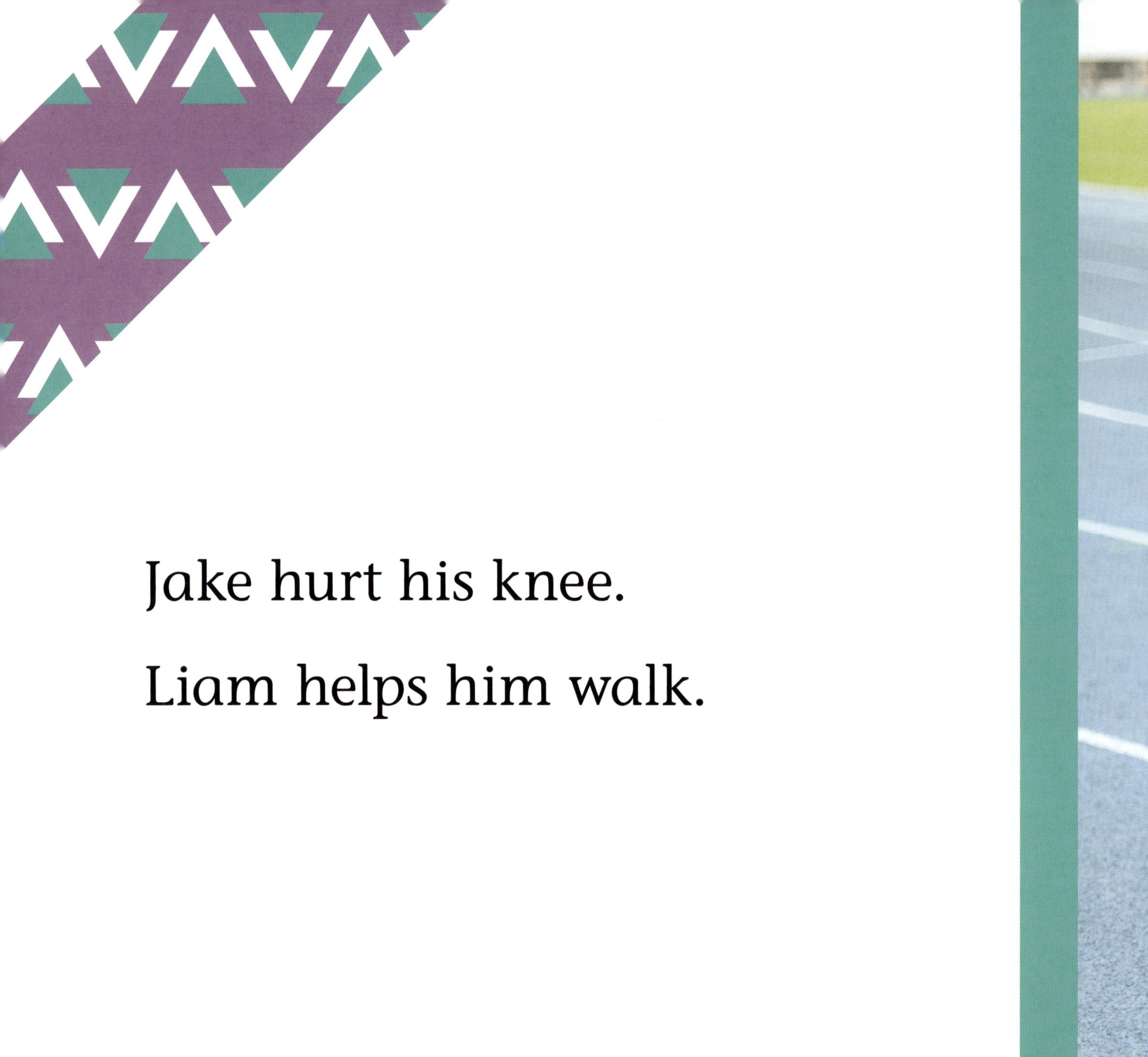

Jake hurt his knee.

Liam helps him walk.

Mae got a puppy.

Ela is happy for her.

Mac's feelings are hurt.

Uma listens to him.

Lisa is **nervous**. Tina helps her.

50
47

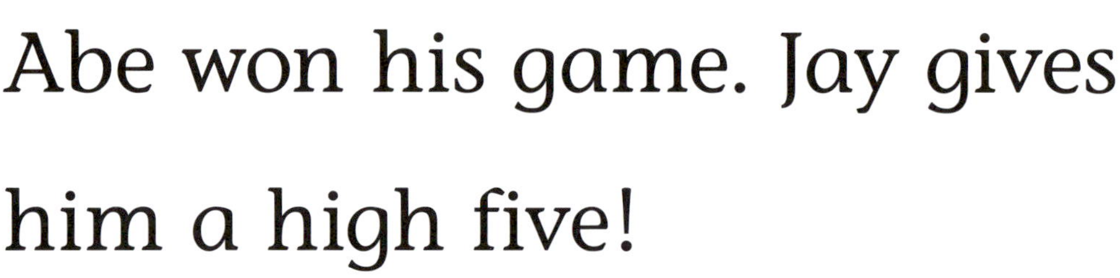

Abe won his game. Jay gives him a high five!

How can you show you care?

Ways to Show Empathy

be a good listener

be happy for others

give a hug

help others

Glossary

nervous
being fearful in a specific situation.

understanding
the ability to understand or to get the importance of.

Index